# Vinazas: The Tequila Industry's Dirty Little Secret

## A Responsible Consumer's Guide to Finding the Best Tequilas to Purchase and Drink

## About The Author

M.A. "Mike" Morales is a tequila tastemaker and agave spirit influencer. His long-running spirits review show on [www.TequilaAficionado.com](www.TequilaAficionado.com), Sipping Off the Cuff, has run for over 1000 episodes and counting, reviewing tequila, mezcal, sotol, raicilla, and bacanora.

His experience and expertise in the agave spirits industry has made him a sought-after consultant, experienced journalist, and significant source for many national and international publications.

Mike has been a life-long bodybuilder and die-hard Dodgers fan, enjoys training table food, good cigars, fine living and traveling with his family, 4 cats and 3-legged dog.

**Find Mike Morales Online**

Personal Website

Tequila Aficionado

Facebook

Twitter

Instagram

Pinterest

LinkedIn

YouTube

## Copyright

Vinazas: The Tequila Industry's Dirty Little Secret By M.A. "Mike" Morales

Published by M.A. Morales

Mike@TequilaAficionado.com

Cover by M.A. "Mike" Morales

**Coming Soon From Mike Morales**

**From Babes to Boss Ladies: Women in the Tequila and Mezcal Industries**

I've had a special place in my heart for the unsung heroines and muses in tequila for a very long time.  After reading <u>Ilana Edelstein's The Patron Way</u>, I felt it was time someone brought other women's stories to light – and what better place to do that than at the leader in tequila

information since 1999 –
***Tequila Aficionado***.
It all began with Tequila Boss
Ladies and grew from there.

## From Babes to Boss Ladies

The contributions of women who
create some of the amazing
spirits we enjoy, direct
production and distillation,
support educational efforts, own
brands we love, and otherwise
contribute to the tequila industry
are often overlooked beyond the
90's throwback bikini-babe

marketing efforts of brands.
From Babes to Boss Ladies digs
deep into the world of tequila and
agave spirits and brings these
ladies' stories to light.

# Dedication

*To the industry legends I once considered heroes who turned their backs on me when I investigated their "dirty little secret".*

*And...*

*To the academics,
environmentalists, and
responsible tequileros who have
supported and provided
information for this report.*

# Contents

# A Call To Action

From August 2 to August 6, 2008, I was invited to join small batch distiller, **David Suro** of tequila **Siembra Azúl**, and a host of other educators and key people studying the cultural, anthropological, historical, and ecological aspects of the tequila industry in the beautiful Highlands of **Jalisco, Mexico**.

We would concentrate on touring distilleries specifically in **Arandas** and **Atotonilco**. David's plan was to gather these brilliant minds together in one place and videotape a round table discussion of the issues currently affecting the **Los Altos** region.

Among the participants was **Doctor of Anthropolgy, José de Jesús Hernández López** (Pepe to his friends) from the

**Centro Universitario de Los Altos.**

He would be, and still is, my guide for this investigation.

In late June 2008, rumor had it that the brand new multimillion-dollar **Patrón tequila** distillery in **Atotonilco, Hacienda del Patrón (NOM 1492)**, had been shut down by authorities.

Local agave growers who supplied **Patrón** with its raw materials were said to be complaining loudly that the company was not buying their agave due to the halt in production. Unconfirmed reports followed in early July that **Patrón** had been only partially disabled; the distillery was bottling, but not distilling.

It was unclear then whether the distillery was now at full strength, but its violation was widely known. **Patrón** had been cited by officials of **Semades (La Secretaría de Medio Ambiente para el Desarrollo Sustentable**, or the

**Department of the Environment for Sustainable Development) Jalisco** state's environmental regulator, for dumping hazardous wastes called **vinazas** into the local rivers and arroyos.

*A by-product of tequila distillation and highly toxic, vinazas should be converted into an environmentally safe and reusable irrigation source.*

Although **Patrón** was accused of not complying with the environmental laws **(normas)** governing the treatment and disposal of these wastewaters, it was commonly felt by industry insiders that it was made the sacrificial lamb due to its high visibility in the new distillery.

**Patrón**'s shutdown hadn't reached the newswires in the **United States**, so the timing was perfect to begin the process of asking questions and seeking answers. I returned to the land of the blue agave, an area that had captured my heart three years before, and investigated the source of these rumors.

What I uncovered when I arrived in **Arandas** was a decades-old secret that had outgrown its hiding place: *vinazas*.

## Vinazas: A Crisis In The Making

From the Eurodicautom,
Webster's New International
Dictionary, second
edition, unabridged (via
http://www.proz.com/):

> *"The residual liquid from the distillation of alcoholic liquors; specifically, that remaining from the fermentation and distillation of beet-sugar molasses...."*

For our purposes in this book:

*"The residual liquid from the distillation of alcoholic liquors, specifically tequila, that remains from the fermentation and distillation of blue weber agave."*

From Ian Chadwick's tequila website:

*"The heads and tails from the second distillation are generally discarded

*without redistillation. The residue (or dregs; vinazas) in the stills from the distillation is also discarded."*

In accordance with the official normas governing the processes of tequila production, tequila must be distilled twice to remove toxic methyl alcohol and aldehydes. With either 100% agave tequilas or mixto tequilas (51% blue agave, 49% other sugars), its impurities are removed.

Not one website dedicated to tequila production, including those belonging to the myriad brands available for sale in the **United States** and **Mexico**, gives more than a mere sentence or two on vinazas disposal. It is simply treated as an afterthought.

To understand the enormity of
the Vinazas Crisis, a review into
its history is necessary.

Wastewater dumping is a problem the alcohol industry faces worldwide. In the sugarcane producing countries of the **Caribbean, Central and South America** where caña, rum, aguardiente, guaro, and cachaca are distilled, and in the wine producing countries of **France** and **Spain**, it has been a decades-old preoccupation.

In his July 20, 2008 column **Apenas Ayer (Just Yesterday)**, Argentinean journalist, **Carlos Páez de la Torre**, wrote of **Federico Schickendantz**, the director of the **Municipal Chemical Office**, and his fears about vinazas.

In his article, **Páez de la Torre** was referring to a report that **Federico Schickendantz** had submitted to the Government of the Province on August 20, 1888, and published in the **"Memoria Municipal"** in 1889, one hundred and twenty (120) years ago.

It reads:

> ***"Schickendantz*** *señalaba la necesidad de 'hacer inocuas las aguas servidas y vinazas de nuestros ingenios, cuyo derrame e introducción en los arroyos y acequias constituyen un verdadero*

*peligro para la salud
pública".*

("**Schickendantz** pointed
out the necessity of
'neutralizing the
wastewaters and vinazas of
our industries whose
discharging and
introduction into the
arroyos and streams
constitutes a very real
danger for the public
health.")

**Schickendantz** affirmed that the harmful elements of the vinazas could be neutralized by using burnt lime.

The wastewaters could then be used to irrigate the cane fields and other crops. He proposed that each distillery have two depositories where the wastewaters and vinazas that were produced in one or two hours could be collected.

There, they would each be treated with the burnt lime.

The wastewaters would be immediately used for irrigation, and the treated vinazas could be safely discharged into the rivers and arroyos.

Where the production of the wastewaters was too abundant for crop irrigation, **Schickendantz** suggested that a drainage system be installed to dispose of the treated excess water directly into the arroyos.

Wisely, **Schickendantz** foresaw great benefits to be derived from his treatment process.

He stated:

> *"...se libraría la población de focos de enfermedades, se conservaría pura el agua de nuestros ríos y arroyos, se impediría el exterminio de los peces"*, y

*"se devolvería a los terrenos los elementos de fertilidad; y, más aún, se aumentaría ésta en alto grado."*

("...the population would be freed from the sources of diseases, the pure water in our rivers and arroyos would be conserved, and the extermination of fish would be impeded," and "those elements of fertility would be returned to the soil at a much higher level.")

On February 21, 2001, **Rubén Moreno Pesqueira**, a member of the **Mexican Tequila Academy**, wrote a scathing editorial on its website, berating the **tequileros** (tequila producers) for their seeming lack of interest in preserving the environment, and called for immediate action.

[http://www.acamextequila.com.mx/noflash/noticias/teqeco.htm]

*"La mayoría de las destiladoras, desde que existen y hasta la fecha, vienen descargando las aguas residuales de vinazas, producto del destilado, sin someterlas al mínimo o total de tratamientos establecidos por la norma oficial mexicana, NOM-001-ECOL-1996, cuyo plazo de*

*cumplimiento empezó a vencer a partir del pasado día el 1 de enero del 2000."*

("The majority of the distilleries since their existence until now, have discharged their vinazas, a by-product of distillation, without submitting them to the total or minimum treatments established by the Norma Oficial Mexicana NOM-001-ECOL-1996 whose deadline for compliance has passed on January 1, 2000.")

**Pesqueira** goes on to accuse the distilleries:

> "*Las descargas de las aguas residuales de vinazas producto del destilado, que son muy agresivas, se hacen a cielo abierto, sin darles conducción o tratamiento alguno, dejándolas correr por gravedad,*

*contaminando el ambiente
y dañando los suelos, ríos y
arroyos por las que
transcurren y a las tierras
bajas en las que se
depositan."*

("The discharging of
vinazas, a by-product of
distillation that is extremely
toxic, is done openly
without any treatment to
freely contaminate the
environment and harm the
soil, rivers and arroyos in

which they flow, as well as the lowlands where they are deposited.")

**Pesqueira** notes that ethical distillers, who are aware of the damage that is caused by the dumping of vinazas, have the financial capability of investing in wastewater treatment facilities without de-capitalizing their operations or production. He holds accountable the larger distilleries that in recent years have been acquired by foreign investors, and that have also inherited the responsibility of investing in wastewater treatment facilities.

For the smaller factories, he suggests that there are banks ready to loan money for 100% of the costs of environmental improvements to their distilleries through special programs funded by the Mexican government for these projects.

Finally, he asks a simple question
of the tequileros,

*"¿Esperar a qué y para
qué?"*

("Wait on what, and why?")

# NOM-001-ECOL-1996: An Explanation

The office of the **Secretaría de Medio Ambiente Y Recursos Naturales** (Secretary of Environment and Natural Resources, or SEMARNAT), is a Mexican federal government agency whose job it is to protect and conserve the ecosystems, as well as to stop and reverse pollution of the water, air and soil.

In 1996, it established the law **(norma)** governing the levels of toxicity allowed in wastewaters and vinazas. These guidelines were to be strictly adhered to by 2000. To date (2009), no distilleries have achieved these levels.

**Semades** (La Secretaría de Medio Ambiente para el Desarrollo Sustentable, or the Secretary of the Environment for Sustainable Development), **Jalisco**'s environmental agency, is in charge of enforcing the compliance of this and other environmental normas. The norma states that chemical oxygen demand (COD) and biochemical oxygen demand (BOD) of vinazas should be only 150 milligrams per liter to be considered non-toxic.

On average, however, a liter of vinazas produces around 52,000 milligrams per liter of COD, and 25,000 milligrams per liter of BOD!

Tequila vinazas is a highly stubborn wastewater. It contains elements similar to those present in the wastewaters of molasses distilleries, most likely due to the white sugar, brown sugar, glucose, fructose or molasses used in the process of mixto tequila (51% agave, 49% "other sugars").

To compound its toxicity, it has a low pH and high temperatures.

Highly colored, as a water
pollutant it blocks out the light to
rivers and streams preventing
oxygenation by photosynthesis
which harms aquatic life.

If dumped on land without any
treatment, it reduces the
alkalinity of the soil and crops are
destroyed.

To top it off, its odor is highly
offensive!

# A Dangerous Loophole

An article by Jesús Estrada Cortés for **Público**, published on April 23, 2008 and reposted on the blog **Verde Bandera (Green Flag)**, declares in its title

> *"Ninguna tequilera cumple NOM del agua"*

> ("No tequila distillery complies with the NOM governing water usage").

In it, the head of **Semades**, **Martha Ruth del Toro Gaytán**, explains an alternative method allowed by the **Comisión Nacional del Agua** (National Water Commission or CNA) for wastewater disposal.

> *"La alternativa que les ha dado la CNA es que las vinazas, con ciertas condiciones de análisis previo de impacto, sean utilizadas para riego en sus*

*propios cultivos, de tal manera que no se estaría incumpliendo con la norma, porque no se arroja de forma directa a cuerpos de agua', explicó la funcionaria, quien agregó que por esto solamente hay 'excepciones' de descargas directas de residuos."*

("The alternative that the CNA has offered is that the vinazas, under certain conditions of analysis prior to impact, can be used for crop irrigation. In this way, it wouldn't be in violation of the norma since there wouldn't be any direct dumping into bodies of water,' explained the official, who added that because of this, there were only 'exceptions' of direct discharging of wastewaters.")

## Throwing Pigs Under A Bus

Between April 24-26, 2008, in an attempt to address the vinazas situation, **Semades**, in conjunction with the **Centro Universitario de Los Altos de la Universidad de Guadalajara**, organized

*"El II Congreso sobre el Manejo Sustentable de la Agroindustria Tequilera"*

(Second Congress concerning the Sustainable Management of the Tequila Agroindustry).

The object of the meeting was to generate technological proposals designed to treat the environmental impact of the tequila industry in the **Los Altos** region, as well as in **Amacueca, Arenal, Tequila**, and **Magdalena.**

Subjects included the implementation of programs to treat sewer drainage of the tequila factories, and the management of vinazas disposal.

Scientists in attendance also explained the complicated chemistry inherent in vinazas.

They suggested solutions to try to reverse the environmental degradation that had occurred in the affected areas.

One of those scientists was my guide, **Dr. José de Jesús Hernández López**.

Although tequileros situated in the affected areas were invited to attend, Pepe confirmed that not one "decision maker or stakeholder" of any of the tequila distilleries participated in the three-day conference.

In the aforementioned **Cortés'** article, **del Toro Gaytán** admits:

*"En estos momentos
ninguna compañía
tequilera cumple con la ley
ambiental en lo que se
refiere a las descargas de
residuos a ríos y lagos..."*

("At this moment none of
the tequila companies
comply with the
environmental law that
refers to the discharging of
wastewaters into rivers and
lakes...")

The article also states that in 2007, 197 distilleries were inspected.

51 had irregularities, and only 2 were shut down.

In what looks like an effort to keep the peace, **del Toro** continues:

> "*...la industria ya está avanzando en la implementación de*

procesos para mejorar sus descargas.' La funcionaria dijo que el incumplimiento de las normas 'no ha sido por una negligencia o una falta de voluntad o de cumplimiento del empresariado', sino que 'el tratamiento de las vinazas es considerablemente más complicado por la gran cantidad de materia orgánica y de azúcares que contiene el agave.' Además de las altas inversiones *necesarias para instaurar la tecnología, que puede llegar a cinco millones de pesos."*

("'...the industry is advancing in its implementation of processes to improve their wastewaters.' The official said that the incompliance of the normas 'hasn't been because of negligence or lack of intention on the part of the industry,' but that 'the treatment of vinazas is considerably more complicated due to the large amounts of organic material and sugars that the agave contains.' Further, the high costs necessary for the implementation of the technology can reach $5 million pesos.")

In an earlier article in July 18, 2007 (**Porcícolas y tequileras, las más**

**contaminantes en Los Altos), del Toro** accused the pork industry, as well as the tequila distilleries, as being the principal problem of watershed pollution in the **Los Altos** area.

Of the 56 plants that were inspected from July 3 to July 6, 2007, 28 were sanctioned.

## Not A New Problem

Over the years, the Mexican press in several of the agave growing and tequila producing regions has kept a close eye on the industry and its water pollution problems. A simple Google search reveals several articles in local town newspapers of tequila distilleries being caught dumping vinazas as far back as October 2004.

Some of the most urgent ones of 2008 were: **"No hay quien** pare la contaminación en la Región Valles" by **Professor Heliodoro Ramirez Hernández (Buenas Noticias**, February 8, 2008).

Here, **Professor Ramirez Hernández** accused the authorities and tequila distilleries of their negligence in contaminating the **Rio Santiago**, even though the Ecological Laws state that each distillery should have its own vinazas processing plant. The only wastewater plant in the area is in **Amatitán**, but it is exclusively for the processing of domestic wastewater, not for the industrial wastewater and vinazas that is dumped into the river by the 15 tequila factories in the area.

**Ramirez Hernández** claimed that:

> *"Los reponsables de esta situación no ponen nada de su parte ni en Amatitán, ni*

*en El Arenal, ni en Tequila,*

*ni en Hostotipaquillo...."*

("Those responsible for this
situation do not offer any
relief on their part. Not
from those in Amatitán, or
in Arenal, or in Tequila, or
in Hostotipaquillo....")

**"Acaba la contiminación con
arroyo de Los Naranjos,"** by
**Francelia Jauregui (Buenas
Noticias, Saturday, March 1,
2008).**

**Benjamin Montes**, Municipal agent for **Los Naranjos** stated that around 40 families were victims of severe contamination of their water source due to two neighboring towns and two tequila distilleries, namely

> "...la taberna de los Landeros y la fábrica La Querencia de Jose Fernández..."

whose wastewaters connect with the arroyo at **Los Naranjos**.

*"Todo se acabo; las vacas que abrevan del arroyo se mueren; el agua baja turbia y hedionda,' expuso."*

("'Everything is gone. The cows that drink from the arroyo die, and the water is turbid and foul-smelling,' he declared.")

**Montes** added that the problem worsens because other medium and smaller distilleries situated in **Tequila** dump their vinazas into the arroyo under the cover of night.

> *"Los hemos visto; no tienen donde descargar sus desechos y los llevan a tirar a ese arroyo, cuando la ley dice que deben tratarlos."*

> ("We've seen them. They don't have anywhere to

throw their wastewater and they bring them to the arroyo when the law says they have to treat them first.")

*"La industria tequilera siguen contaminado,"* afirma **Gustavo Macías (Buenas Noticias, Saturday, March 1, 2008).** Here, federal deputy **Gustavo Macías Zambrano** confirmed that the alcohol and tequila industry has a severe problem. He admitted that meetings

between **Semades** and the tequileros in 2007 hadn't resolved the contamination of watersheds even though there were concrete agreements made.

> *"Pero no sabemos qué está sucediendo; o no les funcionan sus sistemas, o no los operan porque los arroyos siguen contaminados."*

("But we don't know what's happening; either their

systems are faulty, or they don't use them because the arroyos are still contaminated.")

**Gustavo Macías** went on to say:

*"El año pasado estuvimos revisando los sistemas que usa Tequila Sauza; también estuvimos en Tequilas Finos, que considero que es la planta de tratamiento que se adapta bien a las*

necesidades que tienen las empresas pequeñas y medianas. Tambien se visitó El Tequileño, donde nos mostraron el sistema que construyeron. Tequila Cuervo tiene su sistema propio. Pero seguimos viendo que a pesar de lo que nos mostraron, los arroyos siguen igual, contaminados. Hoy seguimos viendo que los arroyos llevan vinazas."

("Last year we inspected the treatment systems used by **Tequila Sauza [NOM 1102]**; we were also at **Tequilas Finos [NOM 1472]**, that I consider the treatment plant that most adapts to the needs of small to medium distilleries. We also visited **El Tequileño [NOM 1108]** where they demonstrated for us the system they constructed. **Tequila Cuervo [NOM 1122]** has its own system.

But even after what they've demonstrated for us, the arroyos still remain the same-contaminated. Today we still see that the arroyos carry vinazas.")

Finally, **Macías Zambrano** suspected that by the end of 2008, there would be sanctions against all industries that did not pre-treat their wastewater, and that these sanctions could be severe.

[Note: As of 2009, the **Buenas Noticias** website where these articles were posted was no longer functioning. Photocopies are available upon request.]

To squelch more tequilero bashing, this article published in **Público's Milenio** column webpage reads,

> *"Tequileros dicen que no están pasivos ante la contaminación"*

> ("Tequileros say they are not passive about contamination").

[Note: Webpage is no longer operational. Copies are available upon request.]

In this August 2008 interview, **Francisco Soltero**, the General Manager of the **Cámara Nacional de la Industria Tequilera (National Tequila Industry Chamber or CNIT** whose purpose is to strengthen and develop the tequila industry by protecting agricultural, industrial and commercial activities related to tequila) confirmed that there were ongoing diverse projects tailored to the size and specific conditions of each distillery.

He alluded to twelve distilleries that were in the process of acquiring funding for the installation of anti-contaminating equipment, as well as an industry leader that had invested millions of dollars in a sophisticated process to produce biofuels.

All Is Not Lost

Experts studying the Vinazas Crisis and officials at **Semades** agree that there is no one easy solution for the proper disposal of vinazas.

Quoted in a **Noti-Arandas** article by **Sergio Antonio Lozano Jiménez**

*"Detallan proceso de saneamiento de ríos"*

("Detailed processes of river sanitization"),

the Director of Ecology for **Arandas**, **Rogelio Alvarez Galindo** explained:

> *"...vinazas...ese es el problema todavía sin solución, porque no hay estudios suficientemente avalados por un laboratorio para poner una planta en cada*

*tequilera y que salga el agua limpia...."*

("...vinazas is a problem that still has no solution because there are not sufficient studies guaranteed by a laboratory to put a [vinazas processing] plant on every distillery to result in clean water....")

**Alvarez Galindo** continues:

*"...yo ya fui a la Ciudad de México y hablé con varios laboratorios muy serios y tienen problemas, porque de cada molienda sale un tipo de vinaza diferente, dependiendo del tipo de agave y de los grados brits, que le llaman ellos, o sea los azúcares, entonces hoy hacen una molienda de cien toneladas y sale con unas características, mañana hacen otra de 50 toneladas*

*y sale con otras
características."*

("...I went to **Mexico** City
and talked with various
serious laboratories and
they have problems because
each milling batch results in
one type of vinazas,
depending on the type of
agave and brix as they call
them, or, in other words,
the sugars. Today they mill
a batch of one hundred tons
and it results in certain

characteristics, tomorrow
they make another 50 tons
and it results in other
characteristics.")

He concludes,

*"Ahorita, para las vinazas
no existe una solución ni
siquiera a mediano plazo."*

("At this moment, for
vinazas, there exists no
solution, not even a
mediocre one.")

[Note: Webpage no longer available. Copies are available upon request.]

Despite the perceived hopelessness, solutions do exist.

As easily as a Google search reveals the environmental crimes of the tequila industry, it just as easily displays viable solutions to the Vinazas Crisis.

A few examples follow:

- Actual plans and schematics served up by chemical engineers from the **University of Guadalajara** [http://sine.ni.com/cs/app/doc/p/id/cs-11288] for a vinazas processing plant.

- A similar one was under construction at **Destiladora San Nicolás (NOM 1440)** during my visit in August 2008.

- A company called **Sisteco-SA** posted on their website a video of their vinazas processing plant for **Fabrica de Tequilas Finos (NOM 1472).**

[Inactive at original publication in 2009. Web domain expired 12/8/08.]

Officials of the distillery were filmed drinking glasses of

successfully filtered wastewater from the plant's drainage pipes.

Not all attempts at building such plants are guaranteed to be successful, however.

On October 24, 2001, **Tequila Sauza (NOM 1102)** laid the cornerstone of what was to be a state-of-the-art vinazas processing plant at **Rancho El Indio**, one of their ranches outside of Tequila.

[http://www.arquired.com.mx/palm/shwNoticia.ared?idNot=7981]

Under the supervision of French biochemist, **Jean Francois Lavigne** who designed the facility, it was to produce electricity, biofuels, as well as potable water safe enough to discharge into the **arroyo Atizcoa**. With an estimated investment by **Sauza** of between $5 to $11 million dollars, it failed miserably.

What was witnessed instead by my guide, **Dr. Hernández López**, was clandestine dumping of vinazas into the arroyo.

Another interesting option submitted to the **Revista Internacional de Contaminación Ambiental** in 2007, conducted by **Gilberto Iñiguez Covarrubias** and **Francisco Peraza Luna** in 2006, is the use of a polyacrylamide (PAM) polymer flocculant. According to the study, vinazas solids contain solid agave particles consisting mainly of cellulose and pectin, along with yeast cells, proteins, salts and organic acids. Solids separation is a common wastewater treatment, and ionic transfer using polymers to coagulate and flocculate the vinazas is the preferred method.

Coagulation is a process of gathering solids that are suspended in the vinazas.

Flocculation is a process that connects coagulated particles into larger masses for easier removal.

As a value-added byproduct, this form of solids separation may yield materials that can be used as fodder feed, as well as composting with agave solids to create a super fertilizer.

The remainder of the liquid could then be used in crop irrigation.

Using vinazas samples from a medley of distilleries **(La Noria [NOM 1494], La Rojeña [NOM 1122], Leyros [NOM 1489], Cascahuin [NOM 1123], and Evolución 501 [NOM 1469])**, Iñiguez **Covarrubias** and **Peraza Luna** determined that using flocculants could efficiently and cost effectively treat vinazas.

However, due to the varying differences in tequila production by each distillery, a standard flocculant dose could not be established.

## Composting

By far, the most popular and creative method of disposing of vinazas is composting. It is particularly suited to small and medium sized distilleries such as the one owned and operated by **Feliciano Vivanco y Asociados (NOM 1414)**.

**Dr. Adolfo Murillo**, producer of **Alquimia tequila (NOM 1468)**, and a leader in organic agave cultivation, explains,

"Because vinazas are very high in organic content, their dumping into rivers or other bodies of water robs the surrounding water of oxygen, which leads to the destruction of the natural flora and fauna."

He explains,

"This is how we have been dealing with vinazas and bagazo [bagasse, pulp]: the bagazo is arranged in long rows, and then soaked in vinazas. The vinazas help to speed up the breakdown and decomposition of the bagazo, turning it into compost which can then be used in the fields as a fertilizer.

We are also looking into using the undesirable alcohols as a fuel, possibly somewhere in the tequila-producing process. The bagazo can also be used as an animal feed (if monitored closely and combined with other feed). As a fiber, it has many uses in cottage industries."

**Dr. Murillo** concludes,

"I believe these and other environmental issues need to be given attention by the industry. If the right uses are found for the waste products, it can be a win-win situation."

Win-win seems to be where **Tequilera Corralejo (NOM 1368)** in **Penjamo** is headed. Instead of discharging the wastewater into the **Turbio River** as it has done in the past, the distillery now diverts the vinazas into two makeshift dams where tapeworms imported from **California** break down the solids into compost.

From there, the fertilizer is used on a recently planted grove of its first 2000 pistachio trees. The resulting water is then used for irrigation.

This project is at once creating a new industry in the state of **Guanajuato**, as well as new jobs for the people of the area.

**Felipe Soto Mares**, producer of **El Perdido tequila (NOM 1420)**, along with a European company, has taken composting a step further.

"In theory the solution my group is working on will neutralize the pollutants in the vinazas," explains **Soto Mares**.

"The same solution can also be sprayed on to the bagasse in compost piles, [and] reduce composting time by 50%. Compost can

then be used as a fertilizer
increasing crop yields by
37%, i.e., corn, tomatoes,
potatoes etc, etc. Imagine!"

**Felipe** continues,

"The resulting compost can
be used as an alternative
revenue source by creating
a new by product packaged
to ship worldwide.
Rendering poor soils,
becoming rich in nutrients
to produce crops in lower

third world countries where
food sources are scarce."


**Soto Mares** emphasizes,


"There is a much larger
picture to consider."

Biofuels

Another option that has been seriously pursued by the sugarcane industry in **Cuba, Spain, Colombia, Chile, Argentina, Peru, Paraguay**, and **Brazil**, is the production of biofuels.

Some recent examples in various industries include: In late 2008, scientists at the **University of Florida** and **Florida International University** announced they were moving ahead with plans to build the state's first cellulosic ethanol plant on land that belongs to sugar giant **Florida Crystals**.

Unlike the controversial ethanol produced from corn in the Midwest-
a process that sent food prices skyrocketing around the globe in the spring of 2008, and saw Mexican agave farmers burn their plantations in order to grow the more profitable crop that

ultimately led to a tortilla shortage--this plant would use sugarcane bagasse.

If successful, the resulting fuel would make the **Florida** sugar growers an energy powerhouse. For years, **Florida Crystals** has been producing its own electricity by burning bagasse and selling the excess back to **Florida Power & Light**.

Similarly, the **Maker's Mark** bourbon whisky distillery has begun using anaerobic digestion that turns waste into biogas.

**Maker's Mark** uses this energy to offset up to 30% of their natural gas use. Situated on a state-certified nature preserve, it also employs state-of-the-art recycling and wastewater treatment.

Reported by **Reuters**, in the Highlands of **Scotland**, a consortium of whisky distillers is investing 35 million pounds to build a biomass-fueled heat and power plant. Using the draff from whisky production (grain solids removed from the mash prior to fermentation) and pot ale (the liquid high-protein residue from the stills) it would produce enough electricity for 9,000 homes.

Part of the project would include a plant that would turn pot ale into concentrated organic fertilizer for local farmers.

Not to be outdone, on January 29, 2009, spirits giant **Diageo** (stakeholders in both **Jose Cuervo (NOM 1122)** and **Don Julio (NOM 1449)**) announced plans to invest 65 million pounds on a bioenergy facility in **Cameronbridge, Scotland**'s second largest whisky distillery. It will supply 80% of the distillery's electricity, and 98% of its steam requirements.

Spent wash (a mixture of wheat, malted barley, yeast and water) will be converted, via anaerobic digestion, into biogas and a biomass fuel source.

It was expected to be operational in 2010.

On January 27, 2009, behemoth beer maker **SABMiller** announced that it would partly fund a five-year multi-million dollar bioenergy project along with 15 other private companies in the **United Kingdom**. The project will focus on using spent grain from brewing as an alternative energy source.

Finally, on January 7, 2009, **Continental Airlines** became the first **US** commercial carrier to fly a Boeing 737-800 partially powered by biofuels derived from algae and jatropha plants in one of its two engines.

The subject of biofuels is not without its critics, however.

In the above **Continental Airlines** example, jatropha, a smelly and poisonous subtropical plant, and algae are both considered sustainable, second-generation biofuels which use a wider range of plants that release fewer emissions than corn ethanol.

Although the experimental flight was a success, **Continental** chairman and chief executive **Larry Kellner** admitted

> "The challenge will be to produce it in an efficient way in the quantities we need."

Currently, adequate supplies, and the facilities to make them, just aren't available, nor is there enough feedstock at the right prices to be competitive with petroleum. It is estimated that it could take a decade before biofuels make up a significant percentage of the fuel used by the airlines.

In the case of **Florida Crystals, Cornell University** Ecologist **David Pimentel** warned that cellulosic ethanol requires too much energy and biomass to produce every gallon.

He explained that a cellulosic ethanol plant would require three to five times more cellulosic biomass to get the same quantities of sugars and starches that corn has.

Quoted in the **Miami Herald** on October 15, 2008, Pimentel said,

> "To get starches and sugar out of cellulosic material, you have to use a strong acid or an expensive enzyme; then you have to stop the acidity using an alkaline."

Pimentel declares,

"That's why there isn't a single ethanol plant in the world that is using cellulosic biomass to produce ethanol. It's because of economics and energy."

He also believes that there isn't enough biomass as one would think, and that ethanol alone won't solve the country's energy problems.

"Agave can bring in the new era of bio-economics giving the world enough clean energy for a peaceful and secure world."

**-Professor Remigio Madrigal Lugo, Ph.D.**, Agricultural Biotechnology

In a stunning report by **Andrew K. Burger** in **RenewableEnergyWorld.co**

**m** (August 7, 2008), **Professor Madrigal Lugo** and a small group of Mexicans from both the academic and private sectors successfully gained funding from **INE** (**Mexico**'s national ecology institute) for an ambitious agave-to-ethanol project.

The high sugar content of the team's enhanced Agave tequiliana plants (some at 27 to 38 Brix, three times that of sugarcane) can yield up to 2,000 gallons of distilled ethanol per acre per year and from 12,000 to 18,000 gallons per acre per year if their cellulose is included (about 14 dry tons of feedstock per acre each year).

In comparison, corn yields approximately 300-400 gallons of ethanol per acre. Soybeans generate a lowly 60 gallons of biodiesel per acre, and sugarcane can produce anywhere from 600-800 gallons of ethanol per acre according to a study by **National Geographic** (October 2007).

An official of **Sapphire Energy of San Diego**, the company that supplied the experimental algae biofuel for the **Continental Airlines** flight, estimates that 3,000 gallons of biocrude per acre per year could be produced.

> "High quality agaves are very good feedstock material for biofuel...for the following characteristics,"

**Madrigal** explained in the article.

"High total sugar density and content; high weight of the fruit and stems; cultivation and harvest cycles of six years; high density of plants per hectare; genetic diversity and high adaptability, low water requirements; $CO_2$ and capture; methane metabolism; soil retention; plant nutrition; products

from inulin; and low
maintenance during
cultivation."

**Madrigal** concludes:

"The use of products
derived from agaves goes
back to pre-Hispanic
cultures. In the present, it is
common to find examples
of these products in
**Mexico** in traditional
beverages like tequila,
mescal and pulque; in

traditional Mexican cuisine;
arts and crafts; and rope
and fibers, among others.
Agave is a class of plants
familiar and part of the
national culture. A project
or program successful in
producing biofuel in
addition to these would
only be a gainful extension
of uses already existing."

With eco-friendly distilleries and
breweries looking to minimize
the environmental impact that

their respective companies cause, and the worldwide consumer desire to drink and to be socially responsible, why isn't every tequila distillery investing in these solutions to the Vinazas Crisis?

In mid-September of 2008, **Dr. José de Jesús Hernández López** (Pepe) interviewed two of the "Founding Fathers of Modern Tequila," **Drs. Leopodo Solis Tinoco** and **Gabriel Espindola Martinez**. With over 36 years of experience in the tequila and mezcal industries, **Solis Tinoco** and **Espindola Martinez** have helped formulate more than a dozen of **Mexico**'s most popular tequilas such as **Espolón, Corazón de Agave, Siembra Azúl, Don Pilar (NOM 1443)**, and others.

The pair vehemently disagreed with the Mexican government persecuting and "santanizing" only the tequila industry when it is adhering most to the normas concerning wastewater treatment. They felt that all alcohol industries responsible for vinazas contamination, including the mezcal, wine, and sotol sectors, should be held accountable.

All sectors should also be integral parts of a common solution. Both concurred that composting was not the answer since the distilleries would never be able to compost the tons of waste produced daily.

Using it as feed was futile because there just isn't enough livestock, either.

As chemists, both agreed that a solution existed, but that the delay was in tequileros not wanting to invest in the costly technology required for vinazas treatment plants.

They estimated that by using certain processes, approximately 40% of the water used in distillation could be reintroduced safely into the environment as treated wastewater, or as gases through a process of evaporation without contributing to global warming.

**Dr. Hernández López** points out, however, that there is an even deeper reason why tequileros resist investing in wastewater treatment plants.

## Vinazas: The New Colonialism

In his published report,

> *"Las Vinazas del tequila: Nuevos usos, viejas practicas en el tratamiento de las aguas residuales del tequila en **Los Altos** de **Jalisco**"*

("Tequila Vinazas: New uses, old practices in the treatment of tequila wastewaters in the **Los Altos** region of **Jalisco**"),

**Dr. Hernández López** reveals that some tequileros resist in investing in vinazas treatment plants because of the age old relationship between the farmer and the **Patrón**.

According to Pepe's report, between 1994 and 2002, tequila **Cazadores (NOM 1487)**, then owned by **Felix Banuelos** and sons, instituted a process by which they artificially inflated the prices of agave.

Using a business model that was later copied by other industries, they split the company into two divisions, industrial **(Cazadores)**, and agricultural **(Agaveros y Ganaderos)**.

While other tequila factories were buying agave from farmers at say, 70 cents per kilo, Agaveros y Ganaderos were paying a dollar per kilo. In turn, that division would automatically sell the agave to **Cazadores** for say 5 dollars per kilo.

Naturally, the farmers would seek doing business with the **Banuelos**es to insure a good price for their crops. This resulted in the family also controlling a surplus of agave that Agaveros y Ganaderos would in turn sell to other tequila factories at even higher prices.

In this way, the **Banuelos**es were able to control agave, and agave prices.

At the cusp of an agave shortage in 1999, there emerged greedy middlemen, known as coyotes, who allied themselves with tequileros to drive down agave prices.

Their introduction into the production chain estranged farmers from tequileros.

**Cazadores** was exempt from
this problem, however.

From the mid-90's, in
appreciation for the agave
farmers' collaboration, the family
would annually throw lavish
parties on the distillery grounds.
Complete with mariachis and
tequila distilled from their agave,
these get-togethers accomplished
two things: it brought the farmer
in closer contact with the
tequilero **(Patrón)**, and it
allowed **Cazadores** to form

stronger ties with certain preferred agave growers.

During one such fiesta in 2002, the current "solution" to vinazas was introduced.

Even though agave plantations were over extended, and the number of agave growers had climbed from only 300 to over 20,000, an agave shortage was projected in 2003 and 2004.

**Cazadores** invited those growers interested in selling their future crops to secure fair prices. At that time, one of their head engineers introduced vinazas "irrigation".

This engineer explained to the agaveros that the treated vinazas was rich in minerals like potassium and other salts.

Instead of dumping vinazas into the rivers and arroyos as they had before, it could now be used as a super nutrient to irrigate their crops.

He even showed them photos of his own family plantation being irrigated with treated vinazas.

During his demonstration, this engineer explained that it would be required that agaveros allow this irrigation on their plantations if they were to remain favored agave suppliers to **Cazadores**.

Not willing to risk losing their favored position with **Cazadores**, those growers in attendance verbally agreed to allow vinazas flooding on portions of their plantations.

In this manner, **Cazadores** was able to dispose up to 50,000 liters per day of vinzas in the first few months of the "program."

Keep in mind that studies on vinazas, and their effect on the environment, were still in their infancy and not yet fully understood.

Within months, several growers witnessed a plague on their agave, the darkening and hardening of the soil, and the strong smell of alcohol. This was enough to cause some of the growers to refuse further irrigation of their crops with vinazas, thus breaking their ties to **Cazadores**.

To keep their crops from being decimated, and to still remain favored suppliers, other growers negotiated for more limited access to their plantations by **Cazadores**' vinazas transport trucks, allowing only certain portions to be flooded.

In 2004, with agave prices plunging, **Cazadores**, now owned by the transnational rum maker, **Bacardí**, and still under the supervision of the same engineers, was now holding their fiestas semi-annually.

Hoping to become favored agave providers, several desperate growers from the **Arandas** area attended and offered portions of their plantations to be flooded with vinazas during the rainy season when it was presumed that the environmental damage would be lessened by the mixture with rain water.

By virtue of being a commodity, subject to supply and demand and free from government intervention, agave is leveraged as a tool by transnational corporations to establish strong farmer-**Patrón** relationships.

It is important to note that in 2004-2005, when other tequila companies refused to pay exorbitant prices for piñas and agave prices plummeted, the **Banuelos**es were already millionaires, and had helped other agaveros become millionaires as well.

Many became tequileros, producing their own brands. To this day, the sons of **Felix Banuelos** gather together with other agaveros at their family restaurant in **Arandas** situated in front of their new distillery, **Hacienda Vieja (NOM 1412)**, and set the price of agave in the Highlands.

# Bacardí: Caught in the Act

Rum giant, **Bacardí**, has a history of polluting the environment. On Tuesday, November 4, 2008, it was reported in **Wine & Spirits Daily** that **Bacardí** struck an agreement with the **U.S. Environmental Protection Agency** on charges regarding water pollution in their **Puerto Rican** operations.

Cited for dumping polluted water
into the **Atlantic Ocean**, and
failure to meet pollutant limits on
various metals, from March 2002
to July 2008, **Bacardí** was
slapped with a $1.55 million
dollar fine and other penalties.

Only one month later, on
Monday, August 4, 2008, during
my excursion with distiller
**David Suro** to the Highlands of
**Jalisco**, I, along with several
others in our party, witnessed the
discharging of close to 19,000

liters of vinazas onto an agave field (see photos).

**Dr. Hernández López** immediately interviewed the driver of the tanker truck, and discovered that he worked for tequila **Cazadores** (**Bacardí**).

The driver confessed that he, along with two other drivers, would routinely make four trips per day, ten times per week, excluding Sundays. They were paid 50 pesos per trip.

The agave plantation was suspected of belonging to a preferred agave provider of **Cazadores**.

When Pepe asked if the vinazas was treated, the driver admitted that they were probably only cooled before being deposited into the tanker for disposal. He had never discharged hot vinazas like other brands had been alleged to be doing, such as the sprawling **El Charro (NOM 1460)** distillery.

The driver informed Pepe that he was under the impression that if he did not discharge the wastewaters directly into a river or arroyo, he was well within the normas.

Then, one of **David Suro**'s cameramen made an important observation. The portion of the plantation onto which he was releasing the vinazas sloped noticeably downward for several yards.

During my visit to **Destiladora San Nicolás**, I was informed by one of the Jimadores I interviewed that plots of land that sloped downward grew smaller agave due to poor water retention by the plants during the rainy season. The water would simply run off into a nearby arroyo that eventually led to one of the rivers in the region.

It was obvious that the agaveros were very deliberate about where they allowed vinazas discharging by the **Patrón**. Rather than risk damage to their higher yielding plantations, growers chose less-than-adequate land.

This meant real estate that naturally sloped toward arroyos and rivers.

Here is where we met the **CAN**'s loophole. Even though the vinazas discharges weren't directly into bodies of water, they eventually reached and contaminated them.

In December 2008, Pepe interviewed a young boy who worked with his father dumping vinazas for **Cazadores**. The boy related that the factory would call his father to work on Saturday nights at ten.

This is significant in that now the discharging was being done clandestinely on weekend

evenings when environmental
officials didn't work!

The boy also testified that the
level of dumping was

> *"hasta que se inunden las
> plantaciones."*

> ("Until the plantations are
> flooded.")

Patrón: "He's the boss, the cool guy."

~ John Paul DeJoria, owner of **Patrón Spirits Company**

On August 2, 2008, an article appeared in the **Noti-Arandas newspaper**,

[The article is no longer posted. Hardcopies are available upon request.], displaying a 32,000 liter tanker truck that had been detained by authorities for dumping vinazas in an arroyo in the **Cerro Gordo** area.

Upon investigation, the tanker was discovered to belong to the **Patrón** distillery in **Atotonilco**. On the accompanying photo, painted on the rear of the tank, were the words

*"Transporta material NO peligroso."*

("Transports NON-hazardous material.")

It was rumored that the wastewater actually came from **Patrón**'s recent acquisition, **Tequila El Viejito (NOM 1107)** considered by the locals as the "whore of distilleries" due to its long history of being bought and sold several times.

The following news report was submitted to **Tequila.net** on August 18,
2008 from the **Guadalajara Reporter**:

"Patron Tequila Distillery Closed for Contamination of Watersheds

"Of 72 tequila distilleries inspected in the last six months, 65 failed to follow state and federal environmental norms in

treating water
contaminated by the
process and the unused end
product of the cooked agave
piñas.

"Although the largest
tequila producers-
accounting for some 80
percent of production-have
invested millions of dollars
in treatment facilities,
many of the 130 smaller
tequileras in the state are
contaminating heavily in

the **Rio Zula** and **Rio Santiago** watersheds.

"One of the most notable culprits is the maker of the highly popular Tequila Patron brand (sold only in the U.S.), a distillery that was closed by authorities after heavy rainfalls caused its holding tanks to overflow into watersheds.

Source:

**GuadalajaraReporter.c
om**"

On September 27, 2008, the
following rebuttal appeared on
Tequila.net:

"Article update: -
9/27/2008 - Letter to the
Editor (added by MrAgave)

"Dear Sir, "I read over the
weekend your report
"Tequila producers

contaminate watersheds," and wanted to clear up an inaccuracy in the article.

Tequila Patron is firmly committed to limiting the environmental aspect of production, and we're proud to say we're at the forefront of the industry on this important issue, investing millions of dollars in equipment and processes to ensure that waste products are properly treated. To that end, one such measure we're recently implemented is a reverse osmosis system to purify our water. While this system was being installed and tested, we did slow production to allow for this.

"At no time has the Patron distillery been closed by the authorities. Like all distilleries in the area, this is an issue we take very seriously.

"**Ed Brown**, president and
CEO, the Patron Spirits
Company, Southlake,
Texas."

To their credit, **Patrón** seems to
be headed in the right direction
ecologically, environmentally,
and even socially.

The sprawling **Hacienda del
Patrón** distillery was purposely
designed to reflect an old world
feel, and reportedly employees
300 women bottlers who are
serenaded by an opera singing
male manager.

Not only had they been alluded to in several of the aforementioned articles as the "industry leader spending millions of dollars on a wastewater treatment facility," but they corroborate this fact on their website:

> "As a pioneer for clean, no-waste industries, **Patron** has revolutionized a waste treatment process that does not contaminate ecosystems. In fact,

compost created from Agave waste is used in the **Patrón** vegetable garden to grow carrots, tomatoes and more!"

During my journey in **Arandas**, I was introduced to a former **Patrón** insider who claimed that **DeJoria** was extremely environmentally conscious and very concerned for the safety and well being of his employees.

He insisted that **Patrón** fully cooperates with the government agencies, and had indeed spent millions of dollars to make **Hacienda del Patrón** a state-of-the-art facility.

This seems to be in agreement with their website, as well:

> "Patron's state-of-the-art facility includes onsite healthcare, childcare, shuttle buses.... The Patron Spirits Company is working

with the local community to
build a school for the
children of the town."

Although that final sentence is in
total contrast to what some
sources had originally told me,
this last excerpt from the website
is even more incredulous:

"Patron is the world's
number one exporter of 100
percent Agave Tequila, and
the facility has grown to
meet the world's demand.

But Patron is still produced in small batches of high quality."

Interviewed in **Beverage World** in December 8, 2008, CEO **Ed Brown** elaborated:

"When we expand, we do it by batch. If we need to increase by another 300,000 cases, we don't just add on to the old equipment, we actually

build another batch area, so
that each area is only
responsible for X amount of
cases and we can keep the
quality of the tequila perfect
every time."

## Patrón: Simply Imperfect?

It is common knowledge throughout the tequila industry that **Patrón** owns four distilleries, including their newest, the disreputable **El Viejito** distillery.

It was also alleged that **Patrón**'s own water source to produce tequila was contaminated with sulfites and unusable.

Although unconfirmed, sources insisted that for some time, **Patrón** had a clandestine arrangement with a high-ranking town official, a prominent agave grower, to monopolize the area's water supply for a certain number of hours each day.

This left the townspeople without water to conduct their daily tasks.

These sources bitterly complained that not only was **Patrón** polluting the local streams, but also taking the town's water and not giving anything back to the community.

Large tequila producers such as **Herradura (NOM 1119)**, **Sauza (NOM 1102)**, and even **Jose Cuervo (NOM 1122)** were known to donate substantial amounts of money for road improvements, schools, and other social programs.

**Patrón** had exhibited zero interest in any of these.

Sources claim the **Hacienda del Patrón** was shut down for a short time; however, many distilleries close and cease operations during the rainy season (June to October).

The roads are muddy and sometimes impassable for workers to get to the distilleries.

It may have been a coincidence, but others don't think so.

What is known is that it is one of the largest devourers of blue agave. As of October 5, 2008, **Patrón** had grown 30.7% in dollar sales and 32% in volume according to **Information Resources, Inc.** (IRI).

**Nielsen** reported that as of October 18, 2008, the tequila colossus had grown 28.5%--both in just 52 weeks!

Since 2005, **Patrón** has
aggressively pursued the Duty
Free market.

It has been so successful, that it
was voted supplier of the year by
duty free operators worldwide.

It is one of the fastest growing
spirits companies in the industry,
and is now available in more than
100 countries and islands around
the world.

COO **John McDonnell**, interviewed in **Wine & Spirits Daily** on November 21, 2008 attributed **Patrón**'s success to increased advertising.

According to **TNS Media Intelligence, Patrón** spent even more in domestic advertising in 2007--$33 million--than tequila juggernaut, **Jose Cuervo.**

In the **Beverage World** article, **Ed Brown** reminisced that when he joined **Patrón** in 2000,

> "The first time I saw the brand, I knew there was something magical about the whole package and the tequila itself."

What **Brown** forgot to mention was that the "magic" was due to the original producer of **Patrón**, **Tequila Siete Leguas (NOM 1120)**, and its proprietary recipe.

After a failed attempt at a hostile buyout of **Siete Leguas**, spearheaded by **DeJoria**'s late partner, **Martin Crowley**--with additional high-powered backup by **Bacardí**-- **Siete Leguas** continued to distill **Patrón** until 2002, when **Hacienda del Patrón** opened for business with a new NOM and recipe.

Finally, if you spent any time at all watching the Democratic and Republican conventions in 2008, you surely couldn't have missed **John Paul DeJoria** riding in the **Patrón Express**, a luxuriously appointed, vintage railroad car and locomotive that ran on biodiesel.

One could only be hopeful that the biofuel that powered the **Patrón** Express was derived from blue weber agave.

Tequila By The Numbers

In January 2009, the **Consejo Regulador del Tequila**

(Tequila Regulatory Council or CRT) announced that a record 1 million tons of agave from 17,500 registered producers were used by 145 distilleries to increase tequila production by 10% from 2007 to 2008 to an astounding 312 million liters.

Distillation of 100% agave tequila made up 20% of that figure at 163 million liters.

Tequila brands are busy cross marketing themselves into every facet of our lives, from t-shirts, to Mexican themed restaurants and tequila bars, to major league sports team sponsorships. Slick websites, bold outdoor advertising, and catchy TV commercials generate constant media hype.

As mentioned above, **TNS Media Intelligence** calculated that **Jose Cuervo**, the largest **U.S.** tequila brand, spent an estimated $30 million in domestic measured media in 2007.

**Patrón** spent slightly more at $33 million.

The **Distilled Spirits Council of the U.S.** (DISCUS) says we can't get enough of the Spirit of **Mexico**.

Tequila imports have increased by almost 50% since 2002. In 2007 alone, Americans bought more than 10 million cases of tequila.

According to **Impact, New York**, estimated sales for the top three tequila brands in 2007 were **Jose Cuervo** at about 3.9 million cases, **Patrón** at approximately 1.6 million cases, and **Sauza** placed third with 1.5 million cases.

Not to be outdone by the competition, **Jose Cuervo** announced on February 5, 2009 that it was expanding the capacity of their flagship distillery, **La Rojeña**, to produce an additional 25,000 liters of tequila per day.

The 240 million-peso investment would allow **Cuervo** to increase sales from 4 to 6 million cases annually.

Currently, worldwide sales of **Jose Cuervo** are 9 million cases per year.

Unfortunately, their adherence to the wastewater normas is only at level A, with their ultimate goal being to reach exact adherence to level C standards with the latest technology.

Imagine how much more quickly and efficiently these gigantic transnational corporations would achieve compliance with the normas if they funneled only a fraction of their advertising budgets toward vinazas processing plants.

The publicity that could be generated from their ecologically sound decisions would be priceless.



Wherever you live, somewhere in the world, it's tequila time.

**Margaritaville** is a place to relax, unwind, and forget about your troubles; everywhere, it seems, except where tequila is produced, and in particular, The Highlands.

According to all the scientific research available, for every liter of tequila distilled, approximately 10 liters of vinazas is produced.

Take any of the sales figures above, multiplied by ten, and you would obtain only an approximation of the wastewaters generated by each tequila maker.

For those more adventuresome, take the final figure of 312 million liters of tequila produced in 2008, and multiply it by 10.

The result is a staggering 2.652 billion liters of vinazas!

As **Dr. Hernández López** put it to me in **Arandas**,

"Where is all that wastewater?"

## The Terror of Terroir

Expounding the virtues of tequila terroir like a vintner and not a tequilero, small-batch distiller **David Suro**, is one of the biggest supporters of maintaining the purity of the Highland's tequila, as well as its flavor profiles and characteristics.

He confesses that one of the secrets of his brand, **Siembra Azúl**, is not only where the agave comes from, but also where it is fermented and distilled.

The **Feliciano Vivanco y Asociados distillery (NOM 1414)** is surrounded by blossoming fruit trees that lend their airborne pollen to the natural yeast in open-air fermentation tanks providing a distinct flavor to the end product.

**Casa Herradura** fiercely protects the grounds of **San Jose del Refugio** so as not to upset the environment for that same reason.

The idea of terroir hasn't escaped other producers.

Both **Ocho tequila (NOM 1474)**, and **Maestro Dobel by Jose Cuervo (NOM 1122)** are asking higher prices for their offerings claiming that each small batch comes from a different agave field.

Hence, each batch or "vintage" will taste slightly different from the next. A pair of Americans from the **San Francisco Bay** area, with the help of **Carlos Camarena** of **El Tesoro de Don Felipe (NOM 1139)** are preparing an agave spirit that will give the GPS coordinates of the exact field where they handpicked the agave!

As explained by **Drs. Sarah Bowen** and **Ana G. Valenzuela Zapata** in their paper **"Geographical indications, terroir, and socioeconomic and ecological sustainability: The case of tequila"** appearing in the January 2009 issue of the **Journal of Rural Studies**, the larger transnational corporations began planting 90% of their own agave instead of buying product from independent farmers in order to avoid dips in production during times of agave shortages.

This resulted in mass commercial cultivation, and the use of pesticides and herbicides, instead of the more traditional growing practices used by agaveros.

The use of these poisons has led to increased soil erosion, water contamination, and higher levels of pest infestation and disease.

For these reasons, brands like **Dos Lunas (NOM 1124)** now claim to be pesticide free.

As explained in the study, the idea of a geographical indication (GI) is that a region's climate, soil properties, and other geographic characteristics produce unique flavors that can't be duplicated anywhere else in the world.

It is designed to increase cultural and historical pride to a region, support independent famers and traditional farming techniques, and to protect the environment.

According to the authors, tequila's GI has failed in every respect.

To compound this issue, the discharging of vinazas, even in nearby fields that have been sacrificed by farmers for that reason, can affect the end product as easily as pollen from citrus blossoms.

In **Dr. Hernández López**'s earlier interview with **Drs. Leopodo Solis Tinoco** and

**Gabriel Espindola Martinez,** they believed that wind currents could carry the evaporating fumes of vinazas for short distances to surrounding agave fields coating healthier agave plants.

If enough coating of the pencas (leaves) took place, it could change the flavor profile of whole fields of agave.

Vinazas fumes evaporating near open-air fermentation tanks

would definitely change the flavor profiles of your favorite brands.

Such an adverse effect would ruin the clever and expensive marketing campaigns geared toward tequila terroir as a selling point.

## The Tequila Trail

Since the mid '90's, an era dubbed in her blog **"el boom de vinazas"** by **Dr. Ana G.**

**Valenzuela Zapata**, the
foremost botanical and
horticultural expert on agaves,
the tequila industry has seen an
incredible surge in worldwide
thirst for the Spirit of **Mexico**.

It culminated in the **United
Nations Educational,
Scientific, and Cultural
Organization** (UNESCO)
naming the **Agave Landscape
and Ancient Industrial
Facilities of the Tequila**

**region** as a **World Heritage site** in July 2006.

To celebrate, the **Ruta del Tequila** was initiated to promote tourism to the area with millions of dollars earmarked for improvements.

In the works are hotels, museums, tours, shops, etc., all along the route that will include the municipalities of **El Arenal, Amatitan, Tequila, Magdalena,** and **Teuchitlan--**

the same areas affected by the Vinazas Crisis.

Under the auspices of the **CRT**, the project is expected to be completed in 2010, with an official launch in April 2009.

Quoted in the **La Jornada** newspaper article

> *"Que los jimadores no sean los últimos beneficiaries del boom tequilero"*

("Jimadores should not be the last ones to benefit from the tequila boom")

on January 9, 2009, **Juan Casados**, president of the **Cámara Nacional de la Industria Tequilera** (CNIT) vowed,

*"Los industriales somos los responsables de preserver algo que es un paisaje blanco, que tiene vida. Nuestro compromiso como*

*industriales es preservar la demarcación geográfica para cuidar el Patrimonio de la Humanidad."*

("We industrialists are responsible in preserving what is a pure landscape, full of life. Our commitment as industrialists is to preserve the geographic demarcation to protect the World Heritage.")

A quick search of the CNIT website [http://www.tequileros.org] reveals that most members are transnational corporations including **Barardí, Cuervo, Brown-Forman (Casa Herradura)** and **Pernod Ricard (Olmeca; Tezón, NOM 1111)**.

It is interesting to note that in all the published news reports concerning the Vinazas Crisis, the "small-to-medium" factories are blamed for vinazas discharging, yet it is the major producers who are caught and cited. To keep its word, the **CNIT** must also take responsibility for the blatant pollution of watersheds throughout **La Ruta del Tequila** by these transnational corporations.

Otherwise, imagine the mortification of Mexican tour guides on **La Ruta del Tequila** answering this question posed by curious, camera-toting turistas:

"What's that smell?"

## Consumers Make All the Difference

In answer to the demands of consumers abroad, and to pressure from those living in the affected municipalities of the **Los Altos** region, on December 11, 2008, the **Comisión Estatal del Agua de Jalisco** (**Jalisco** State Water Commission or CEA), the **CRT** and the **CNIT**, entered into an agreement to find a solution for the treatment of vinazas.

It provides for the construction of wastewater treatment plants in **Arandas, Atotonilco, Amatitan**, and **Tequila**, to capture the vinazas of "small-to-medium" sized distilleries.

Quoted in a **CEA** press release, department head, **César Coll Carabias**, declared,

*"Este convenio...representa un enorme avance en el tema de 'consciencia" y de*

'responsabilidad' con nuestro medio ambiente y con la cuidadania, de reconocer que, con la elaboración de nuestros productos también hemos contribuido a la terrible contaminación que está terminando con nuestros cuerpos de agua."

("This agreement...represents an enormous advance on the topic of consciousness and responsibility with our environment and with the public in recognizing that, in the elaboration of our products, we have contributed to the terrible contamination that is putting an end to our bodies of water.")

Whether this agreement actually accomplishes its goals remains to be seen.

Some "small-to-medium" distilleries with vinazas treatment plants have been cautiously outspoken in their belief that this agreement is just mere lip service to keep environmentalists momentarily satisfied.

In the tequila industry's largest market, **U.S.** consumers and avid collectors still tirelessly pursue ever more stunningly beautiful and expensive bottles.

But they are also seeking "greenovations," eco-friendly products that allow them to imbibe and to be socially responsible at the same time.

Small batch distillers, whose tequila production is far lower than the mammoth transnationals, are rapidly gaining acceptance.

Companies like the organically certified **4 Copas (NOM 1457)**, USDA certified organic **Casa

**Noble (NOM 1137)** and **3 Amigos (NOM 1499)**, as well as **Alquimia's (NOM 1468)** more traditional agave growing "organic protocols," are taking the alcohol industry's catch phrase "drink responsibly" to a whole new level.

These solutions to the Vinazas Crisis aren't perfect.

As one distillery representative admitted,

"...we must get better."

The care and cultivation of agave, and the subsequent proper disposal of its poisonous vinazas, must take center stage for the tequila industry, its people, and the environment to survive.

If tequila is truly the cultural symbol of **Mexico**, then vinazas must also be representative of its culture. And if that is the case, then what does it signify to the rest of the world?

## Who Is The Real Bad Guy Here?

This was not an easy report to write. At great expense to myself personally and professionally, it has been a labor of blood, sweat, tears, and ultimately, love; love for the "Spirit of **Mexico**," its people, and the land where it originates.

What started as an investigation of rumors that the powerful **Patrón** distillery had been allegedly closed in June or July of 2008 for watershed pollution turned into a report of monumental proportions.

I was accused of "sensational journalism" and ostracized by industry "yes-men" (and women) but my motives were those of a responsible consumer, passionate about tequila.  I was even the victim of industrial espionage when the computer on which I drafted this research was stolen at a popular and well-established tequila show in which I was a judge.

For those of us who have been blessed to visit the tequila and agave growing regions of **Jalisco** and have grown to appreciate the fine tequilas that are produced there, the idea of an environmental polluter the size of **Patrón** was an affront to everything we aficionados hold dear about **Jalisco** and its people.

To have the stark beauty of the Highlands and the Lowlands strangled by a toxic sludge that has reached crisis levels should frighten all of us, from the casual consumer to the diehard purist.

When I saw first-hand the destruction that liters of vinazas can do to the noble blue agave plant and the deep red soil of **Arandas**, my heart sank.

When I witnessed the decimation of rows of agave, the polluting of water sources, and the destruction of the environment, I could not sit idly by.

I felt that would have made me just as reprehensible as those who are responsible for years of devastation to the **Paisaje Agavero**.

To be honest, this project began as a crusade against the bad guy.

As you may have discovered, it's difficult to know who the bad guys are when just about everybody is an active participant.

Whether it's due to bad politics, poor leadership, expert marketing, or just plain greed, the Vinazas Crisis, like agave gluts and shortages, cannot and should not be ignored. Yet, you also read about practical and very viable solutions to this problem.

Money is not the only
commitment needed to
implement these solutions.

It may be a purported obstacle,
but the profits from the cases sold
by the large transnational
corporations that spearhead the
tequila industry are just as
staggering as the figure of vinazas
produced by them in 2008.

At what cost have tequila
companies competed against one
another in an effort to outdo their

production and sales
performances year after year?

They've abandoned their own
people who, in many cases, work
for them and must endure
without clean water.

Jimadores, farmers and other
skilled laborers continue to make
their way into the **United States**
for a better life. These
journeymen, who have worked
their trades for generations, have
been displaced by commercial

cultivation of agave by transnational corporations.

The use of pesticides and herbicides by these corporations are ruining the land and water table.

Add to that the discharging of billions of liters of vinazas, and you have a crisis of pandemic proportions no less serious than the Ebola virus!

What is necessary is a commitment by small batch distillers, environmental officials, academia, and discerning consumers to heed the calls for help by the people of the **Paisaje Agavero** who suffer as a consequence of this unconscionable polluting.

## What You Can Do

If you are planning to visit **Mexico** "in search of the blue agave," I encourage you to discover for yourself what distilleries are doing with their wastewaters by asking questions.

Tequileros with nothing to hide should be just as proud to show you their wastewater treatment facilities as they are their fermentation tanks and laboratories.

If you have visited tequila distilleries in the past and have fallen in love with the sights, sounds, scents, flavors and traditions of the Highlands, the Lowlands, and its people, you'll agree that the experience is euphoric and life altering.

But, imagine the sweet smell of cooked maguey and damp barrel rooms overcome by the putrid stench of vinazas as it chemically

burns the rotting blue agave in
the fields.

I urge you to hold these
environmental criminals
accountable, whoever they may
be.

When you observe what you feel
is a crime against the
environment and the individuals
who inhabit it, say so.

Alert other consumers to the fact
that there is more to tequila than

just a pretty bottle, or a shot with lime and salt.

As a knowledgeable consumer, send a message to those who market and sell those pretty bottles that you won't stand for anything less than full, ecological responsibility of the spirits--and the spirits companies-that you choose to patronize.

It is up to the socially conscious, ecologically minded, environmentally active tequila and/or spirits consumer to up level the catch phrase "drink responsibly."

In sharing the information in this book, it is my hope that next time you reach for your favorite brand of tequila at your local store that you are mindful of the decision you're making.

Is your brand eco-friendly, or are you directly contributing to the uncontrolled watershed pollution of the **Paisaje Agavero** by

supporting your brand's total
disregard for the environment?

I also hope to inspire you to
become conscious of the impact
of your buying decisions.

The Vinazas Crisis deserves your
attention.

The time has come to not only
drink responsibly, but to also
think responsibly and purchase
accordingly.

*Sip wisely.*

www.ingramcontent.com/pod-product-compliance
Lightning Source LLC
Chambersburg PA
CBHW061336250726
48657CB00004B/1197